D1710778

GET A JOB

AT THE
LANDFILL

JOE RHATIGAN

Created and produced by
Bright Futures Press, Cary, North Carolina
www.brightfuturespress.com

Published by
Cherry Lake Publishing, Ann Arbor, Michigan
www.cherrylakepublishing.com

Photo Credits: cover, Shutterstock/Minerva Studio; page 4, Shutterstock/kanuag; page 5, Shutterstock/Paul Vasarhelyl; page 7, Shutterstock/Jarvek Chairak; page 7, Shutterstock/Dmitry Kalinovsky; page 9, Shutterstock/bokan; page 11, Shutterstock/marino bocelli; page 11, Shutterstock/VERTIGO Creative; page 13, Shutterstock/bibiphoto; page 15, Shutterstock/marinobocelli; page 15, Shutterstock/bokan; page 17, Shutterstock/north allertonman; page 19, Shutterstock/ Alexey Stiop; page 19, Shutterstock/Adam Gregor; page 21, Shutterstock/sima; page 23, science photo; page 23, Shutterstock/Comaniciu Dam; page 25, Shutterstock/Avatar_023; page 27, Shutterstock/LYSVIK PHOTOS; page 27, Shutterstock/TFox Foto; page 28, Shutterstock/ChiccoDodiFC.

Illustrated by Chris Griffin

Library of Congress Cataloging-in-Publication Data

Names: Rhatigan, Joe, author.
Title: Get a job at the landfill / by Joe Rhatigan.
Description: Ann Arbor, Michigan : Cherry Lake Publishing, 2016. | Series:
    Get a job | Audience: Grades 4-6. | Includes index.
Identifiers: LCCN 2016008206| ISBN 9781634719056 (hardcover) | ISBN
    9781634719513 (pbk.) | ISBN 9781634719285 (pdf) | ISBN 9781634719742
    (ebook)
Subjects: LCSH: Refuse and refuse disposal--Juvenile literature. | Waste
    disposal sites--Juvenile literature. | Sanitation workers--Juvenile
    literature. | Fills (Earthwork)--Juvenile literature. | Recycling (Waste,
    etc.)--Juvenile literature.
Classification: LCC TD792 .R53 2016 | DDC 363.72/8--dc23
LC record available at http://lccn.loc.gov/2016008206

Printed in the United States of America

TABLE OF CONTENTS

Dealing with garbage isn't just smelly business, it's BIG business.

Not too long ago, everyone's garbage was delivered to a dump and left to stink up the place. Today's garbage is sorted, recycled, reused, and compacted, and in some cases, is sold for profit! **Landfills** use science and technology to create more environmentally responsible solutions for how to get rid of our **waste**. And the people who deal with our trash work hard, so we don't have to think too much about our garbage once it's picked up from our homes and businesses.

What are some of the interesting jobs in the waste management industry? Let's find out by following the garbage created by **J**eremiah **O**liver **B**aumgartner. (His parents and friends like to call him by his initials: J.O.B.) Job isn't a real kid, but the people who work with his garbage represent real professionals found at landfills everywhere.

By the end of this book, you'll be glad to know that the many people who work at the landfill are on the job. Who knows? You may even decide that working with garbage is pretty amazing!

FUN FACT
The waste industry employs nearly 400,000 people.

"Job, your room looks like a landfill," Mom said.

"Don't even think about going outside with your friends until your room is clean!"

For some kids, that might take 45 minutes or less. But not Job. "Oh man, I'll be an old man before I get this mess cleaned up!"

When Job finally finished, he had a collection of junk. What was he supposed to do with a bunch of sticks left over from an art project? And the almost-empty can of paint? And all of his social studies handouts from last year? Plus the soda can that had spilled out all over the floor...

It's not *that* bad, right, kitty?

... *Meow?*

Most homes and businesses place their garbage in cans, or bins, for pickup. **Drivers** are responsible for picking up trash and delivering it to a transfer station or landfill or **incinerator**. A driver may operate a sanitation truck for home pickup, a larger front-loader for business pickup, or a large roll-off truck to pick up **dumpsters**. This physically-demanding job requires attention to detail and safe driving skills.

Curbside pickup keeps communities conveniently trash-free.

The **sanitation helper** works alongside the driver, hauling trash cans to the sanitation truck, emptying the containers, and returning them to the curb. This is also a physically demanding job that requires safe lifting practices in order to not get hurt.

The **dispatcher** works in an office and uses a radio system to stay in contact with all the sanitation drivers out on the road. The dispatcher schedules pickup service, gives drivers their pick-up routes for the day, and makes sure garbage is picked up in a timely fashion. The dispatcher also schedules special pickup service for oversized items and hazardous materials.

Teamwork and big trucks get the job done!

Whew! I'm definitely getting a workout today!

The **recycling driver** and **recycling helper** operate a special truck that is used just for picking up materials that can be recycled. These items include cardboard, plastic containers, paper, glass, and more. They drive their full trucks to transfer stations or recycling-sorting areas. Currently less than 35 percent of households and less than 10 percent of businesses in the U.S. recycle. People who work in recycling will be even busier as more people do their part and recycle more.

The drivers, helpers, and dispatcher report to the **route supervisor**, or manager. This person oversees the daily service delivery to the customers. He has to make sure drivers are following safety regulations and picking up the trash on time. The supervisor also has to make sure all operations stay within budget.

THE RESULTS

Job placed the sticks on top of some leaves for yard-waste pickup day. He washed out the soda can and put it in the recycling bin along with all the old homework.

Job's dad called the dispatcher to schedule a hazardous materials pickup for the paint can and some other chemicals that had been sitting in the garage.

Job looked at the piles in front of his house. "All I did was move the landfill from my room to the curb!"

Job watched his garbage disappear from the curb.

"Well, that's that!" Job said. "It's gone, and I don't have to worry about it anymore."

But then he began to wonder what a landfill really looked like, and where his garbage actually went. Turns out it was his lucky day. His mother was filling the trunk of the car with a big pile of old magazines and newspapers.

"I'm making a run to the city landfill," she said. "Come along and bring your garbage."

"But I got rid of all my garbage already," Job said.

"Did you clean under your bed?" Mom asked.

"Oh, yeah ..."

Some communities have a **transfer station**, which is a site where garbage trucks drop off their daily loads. This garbage is then put on bigger trucks bound for the landfill. A **transfer station attendant** or manager will make sure all the garbage dropped off is placed on the right trucks. The attendant may also act as a dispatcher, scheduling drop-offs and deliveries. Some transfer stations allow customers to drop off their garbage, which comes in extremely handy when people clean out their garages or get ready to move.

Customers entering a landfill stop at the entrance, where the vehicle carrying their garbage will be weighed by the **scalehouse attendant**. The customer has to pay for the garbage being dropped off, which is why it is weighed. The attendant must check loads and figure out the payment due. This worker also makes sure anyone who enters the landfill area follows all safety rules and isn't bringing items not allowed at that landfill.

Safe drivers needed!

Garbage is dropped off at one small portion of a landfill, called a cell. A **compactor operator** smashes the trash with a large truck called a compactor. The operator runs over the garbage and squashes it until it's as small as possible, which makes room for more garbage. The operator may also get to drive other trucks on the landfill such as scrapers, bulldozers, backhoes, and more.

One of the more important jobs at the landfill is the **mechanic**. A landfill can only operate well if all its equipment is working, and it's the mechanic's job to make sure that happens. Whether it's a truck, pump, or monitoring device, mechanics have the know-how to maintain and fix all the equipment if it breaks.

Mechanics keep landfill equipment running smoothly.

The **landfill laborer** performs many duties during the day. He may pick up garbage that blew away from the landfill, help mechanics fix machinery, and clean and refuel the trucks. He also might perform janitorial work at the office and help separate garbage at transfer stations. This job is a great entry-level position that provides lots of great training, skill development, and life skills that can lead to better opportunities down the road. Many a landfill professional got their start this way!

THE RESULTS

The landfill fascinated Job. He was also surprised that it didn't smell that bad, even though there was trash everywhere. He watched the garbage from under his bed get thrown into a cell at the landfill, and then crushed by a compactor. Smoosh!

"Wish we had one of those at home," Job said.

"Yeah," Mom said. "We could use it for your room."

Yard Waste

Household Waste

Recycling

I was hoping they'd have directions to the snack bar.

The landfill had many different sections, with areas for various kinds of trash.

Trees, leaves, and bushes were delivered to one area, recyclables went to another. Piles of garbage surrounded Job, everywhere he turned!

"Where does all this trash come from?" he asked.

"Places around us, like houses, businesses, and even construction sites," Mom said.

"This place sure is a dump!" Job said.

"You can say that again," his mom said.

"Okay," Job answered. "This place sure is a dump."

Large roll-off trucks unload garbage from construction sites, such as wood, metal, and cardboard. The **building materials recovery operator (BMR)** is in charge of this area. The BMR works with others to empty the trucks, sort the materials, and place them in the correct piles. The BMR operator transports the wood to the **composting** area of the landfill (or sends it to a composting business), sells the metal to dealers who will reuse the metal, and sends the cardboard to paper recyclers. Any Styrofoam or other material that can't be recycled ends up in the landfill.

Recycling centers sometimes operate at the landfill—or a different company may handle the community's recycling. There are many jobs at a recycling plant, but the **recycling supervisor's** job is to make sure that the site is working up to capacity and that everyone is doing their job. These jobs include unloading garbage, sorting through the recycling once it's dumped onto conveyor belts, and baling cardboard and paper. The supervisor also makes sure that all regulations are being met, including staying safe!

Supervisors make sure all rules are followed.

There are certain types of garbage you don't want in the landfill. Batteries, old paint, chemicals, cleaning supplies, and other hazardous materials need to be separated, so they don't contaminate the water that drains down through the landfill. This could pollute the community's drinking water. The **hazardous materials specialist** knows how to move and get rid of this dangerous garbage. A hazmat professional knows the laws and disposes of these materials in a way that won't harm people, animals, or plant life. In most cases, this specialist separates the different dangerous materials, seals them into

Safety first when dealing with hazardous waste.

containers, and gives them to companies that deal with proper disposal. This position may also require inspecting garbage when it is delivered to the landfill, making sure any hazardous materials are removed.

Oh man! Even I couldn't drink this much soda.

For communities that have yard waste and food waste pickup, the landfill, or a company hired to do the job, will use these materials to make mulch or soil. A **compost technician** helps push wood waste into a grinder and mix the wood pieces with biosolids from the wastewater plant. (Also known as processed poop!) The pile of wood and poop is kept at the proper temperature and moisture level until it is ready to be used at parks and on yards. Food waste is handled in a similar way to make compost or new soil.

THE RESULTS

The recycling area was Job's favorite part of the landfill. He liked wondering what kinds of new stuff all that trash would be used to make.

"Now, this is what I call 'trash talk'," Job's mom said.

"Well, actually," Job said, "It's more like 'recycle talk'."

Recycle Up
Landfill Down

Job's hometown was lucky to have a modern landfill that helped protect the environment and worked to reduce and reuse waste.

His community landfill was known as a "wet" landfill, because it composted the garbage in the landfill instead of just containing it.

"Maybe I should compost in my bedroom." Job said. "Then I wouldn't have to clean up so much."

Pfffew! Smells worse than my gym bag.

More and more landfill operators are looking for new and exciting ways to reuse garbage. One such way is to trap the gases the landfill produces and turn it into energy. As the garbage **decomposes** and begins to break down, a gas called **methane** is released. A **landfill gas technician** monitors the methane that's produced and operates the machinery and tanks that collect the gas. Methane can be sent to power plants for electricity, or piped to an energy company to use for heating.

Water that enters a landfill ends up becoming contaminated. This water must be prevented from soaking into the ground where it can end up in our drinking water. This "trash water" is called **leachate**, and a **leachate technician** maintains the system of pipes that collect the water. The water is pumped to a treatment plant, where it is cleaned and returned to the landfill, or sent elsewhere. The leachate technician monitors the process and makes sure the leachate doesn't build up in the landfill.

Environmental technicians keep their eyes on the big picture when it comes to finding new and better ways to reduce and reuse the garbage that ends up at the landfill. They sudy existing practices, looking for ways to improve them, and research new garbage treatment technologies. These technicians will also sample waste material and study lab results, to make sure the landfill is not contaminating the ground and water.

Machinery like this is used at landfill gas recovery plants.

Overseeing all this activity is the **landfill operator**, also known as the general manager. A landfill operator makes sure the landfill is properly operated with **permits** in place, and all safety, environmental, and equipment polices are being followed correctly. There are a

Technicians test for "trash water."

lot of laws limiting what a landfill can do. The landfill operator has to make sure everything is in order. Problems can cause poisonous drinking water, uncontrollable smells, or hurt employees.

THE RESULTS

After an interesting day at the landfill, Job and his mom drove home. Along the way, Job noticed garbage cans, dumpsters, plastic garbage bags, and even litter, just about everywhere he turned.

"This whole garbage business is a lot bigger than I ever imagined," he said. "I wonder what our town would look like if all these people we met today didn't do their jobs?"

Before his mother could answer, Job said, "I know, I know. It would look like my room!"

Seeing people litter really makes me feel down in the dumps.

CHAPTER 5

JOB RECYCLES

Job wasn't done thinking about garbage.

He looked up more jobs that deal with garbage and landfills and was surprised to find dozens of different types of businesses that deal with trash, even if they're not close to a landfill.

There are jobs in garbage that don't smell as bad, Job thought.

But Job couldn't get the recycling idea out of his mind. He emptied the contents of his trash can onto the floor and stared at it, thinking about what he could make from it.

Let's see what I can make. Besides, a mess, I mean.

A **waste auditor** is hired by a business to measure the amount and type of waste the business produces, so it can make improvements. The auditor will visit the site, watch how people deal with waste, and monitor the recycling. Once the auditor has the necessary data, he or she creates a plan that can help improve recycling rates at the business, and perhaps get it certified as a Zero Waste contributor. That means the business recycles or reuses nearly all the waste it produces.

A third-party **electronics recycler** works with one sort of garbage most people think about: electronics. This includes old computers, cell phones, and wires. Electronics recyclers buy these goods from landfills and other businesses. They remove as much of the metals and other materials as possible, and then sell these materials for a profit. Many of these materials are sold back to the companies that make computers and cell phones.

One item that can be a pain for landfills to deal with is metal, which doesn't decompose in the landfill. You can crush the metal so it takes up less space, but it will remain in the landfill forever. A **scrap metal broker** buys metal garbage from landfills and junkyards, and sells it to another business, where it will be turned into new products.

One man's trash is another man's treasure!

Have you ever had a great idea that you knew would make millions of dollars? An **entrepreneur** is someone who does just that. Many entrepreneurs look for ways to reuse garbage. Entrepreneurs have turned plastic bottles into thread that is used to make grocery bags and even clothes! They buy old car tires and turn them into asphalt or basketball courts.

Many scientists enter the field of waste management. **Environmental scientists** use their knowledge to

Who knows where the next big idea in recycled trash will come from?

help protect the environment. They may help clean up contaminated areas or work with different businesses to help reduce pollution and waste. If there's a possible environmental disaster somewhere, environmental scientists will investigate and come up with an action plan. Chemists, biologists, physicists, and lots of other people also work to create solutions for dealing with our garbage.

THE RESULTS

Job told his dad all about their day and showed what he made out of his recycled trash.

"One man's garbage is another man's treasure," his dad responded.

Job thought more about it. "I guess, just because I don't want something doesn't mean it's not valuable," Job said. "And just because someone works with garbage doesn't mean that job stinks."

WHO DOES WHAT?

Job met some interesting people during his landfill adventures. Can you match their job titles with the correct job descriptions?

Please do NOT write in this book if it is not yours. Use a separate piece of paper.

1. Person who buys metal from landfills and junkyards and sells the metal to businesses to make new products

2. Person who makes sure the landfill is as environmentally-friendly as possible

3. Person who operates a special sanitation truck to pick up recyclable materials

4. Person who keeps sanitation trucks and equipment in good working order

5. Person who safely disposes of batteries, old paint, cleaning supplies, and other chemicals

A. Mechanic

B. Recycling driver

C. Hazardous materials specialist

D. Scrap metal broker

E. Environmental technician

Answer Key: 1-D; 2-E; 3-B; 4-A; 5-C

WHO? WHAT? WHY?

Choose the correct job title to complete the sentences below.

1. A _____ measures the amount and type of waste generated by a business.

2. A _____ uses a radio system to stay in touch with sanitation drivers on the road.

3. A _____ operates the trucks that compact trash at a landfill.

4. A _____ makes mulch or soil out of yard waste.

5. A _____ is in charge of running the landfill.

A. compactor operator

B. dispatcher

C. landfill operator

D. compost technician

E. waste auditor

Answer key: 1-E; 2-B; 3-A; 4-D; 5-C

Hey, Job here! Now that you've read all about my landfill adventures, it's time for your story.

Write a story about your own adventures in trash and recycling. Be sure to mention the people you've seen working in waste management in your community.

Pssst ... If this book doesn't belong to you, write your answers on a separate sheet of paper so you don't get in BIG trouble.

Go online to download a free activity sheet at **www.cherrylakepublishing.com/activities**.

GLOSSARY

biodegraded
broken down by natural processes

building materials recovery operator (BMR)
person who sorts and separates the garbage delivered from construction sites

compactor operator
worker who drives a compactor that smashes the garbage delivered to landfills so it doesn't take up as much space

compost technician
person who works on turning the wood waste delivered to a landfill or other facility into mulch and compost

composting
where organic matter has been decomposed and recycled as soil

decompose
to rot or decay

dispatcher
person scheduling the sanitation workers who are picking up curbside trash

drivers
people who drive sanitation trucks and pick up trash in front of homes and businesses

dumpster
the name of a large trash container that is lifted and emptied into a truck

electronics recycler
someone who buys old electronics, breaks them down into their basic materials, and then sells the materials for a profit

entrepreneur
someone who starts a business that sounds like a risky idea at the time

environmental scientist
scientist who works to protect the environment

environmental technician
worker who finds new and better ways to reduce and reuse the garbage that ends up at a landfill

hazardous materials specialist
worker who collects and properly disposes of chemicals and other items that are too dangerous to put in a landfill

incinerator
an apparatus for burning waste material at high temperatures until it is reduced to ash

landfill
place where garbage and other waste material is disposed of

landfill gas technician
worker who monitors the methane that's produced by a landfill and operates the machinery that's used to collect the gas

landfill laborer
worker who performs many duties at a landfill such as picking up trash, helping mechanics, and refueling trucks

landfill operator
worker who is in charge of the landfill facility and makes sure the landfill is operating safely while following all the rules and regulations

leachate
the contaminated trash water collected from landfills

leachate technician
person who maintains the system of pipes and tanks used to collect and clean leachate

mechanic
worker who maintains and fixes the many trucks and equipment at a landfill

methane
a colorless, odorless, flammable gas that is released during the decomposition of plant or other organic compounds

permits
official documents giving someone permission to do something, such as operate a landfill

recycling driver
worker who operates a special sanitation truck that picks up only items that can be recycled, such as glass, plastics, and paper

recycling helper
person who helps haul recycling materials to the truck

recycling supervisor
person who oversees the operations at a recycling plant

route supervisor
worker who oversees the daily service delivery to customers

sanitation helper
worker who hauls garbage to a sanitation truck and empties the containers

scalehouse attendant
person who weighs the trash that comes into the landfill in order to charge the drivers of the trucks or the company delivering the garbage

scrap metal broker
someone who buys metal from landfills and junkyards and sells it to other businesses for a profit

transfer station
a building or site where garbage trucks drop off their garbage

transfer station attendant
worker who ensures that dropped-off garbage is placed on the right trucks for delivery to a landfill

waste
garbage created by humans

waste auditor
worker who helps companies reduce waste

INDEX

ABOUT THE AUTHOR

Joe Rhatigan is an accident-prone author whose works include *Ouch! The Weird & Wild Ways Your Body Deals with Agonizing Aches, Ferocious Fevers, Lousy Lumps, Crummy Colds, Bothersome Bites, Breaks, Bruises & Burns*; *White House Kids*; and *Inventions That Could Have Changed the World, But Didn't*. He lives in Asheville, North Carolina, with his wife and three kids.